Mothersalt

Mothersalt

MIA AYUMI MALHOTRA

Alice James Books
NEW GLOUCESTER, MAINE
alicejamesbooks.org

10 9 8 7 6 5 4 3 2 1

Alice James Books are published by Alice James Poetry Cooperative, Inc.

Alice James Books
Auburn Hall
60 Pineland Drive, Suite 206
New Gloucester, ME 04260
www.alicejamesbooks.org

Library of Congress Cataloging-in-Publication Data

Names: Malhotra, Mia Ayumi, author.
Title: Mothersalt / Mia Ayumi Malhotra.
Other titles: Mothersalt (Compilation)
Description: New Gloucester, Maine : Alice James Books, 2025.
Identifiers: LCCN 2024054979 (print) | LCCN 2024054980 (ebook) | ISBN
   9781949944723 (trade paperback) | ISBN 9781949944945 (epub)
Subjects: LCSH: Motherhood--Poetry. | LCGFT: Poetry.
Classification: LCC PS3613.A4356 M68 2025 (print) | LCC PS3613.A4356
   (ebook) | DDC 811/.6--dc23/eng/20241129
LC record available at https://lccn.loc.gov/2024054979
LC ebook record available at https://lccn.loc.gov/2024054980

Alice James Books gratefully acknowledges support from individual donors, private foundations, the
National Endowment for the Arts, and the Poetry Foundation (https://www.poetryfoundation.org).

Cover image: "Celestial Blue" by Yoshi Nakagawa

CONTENTS

THREE

for my daughters

WHERE POEMS COME FROM

Could be from under a duck's wing, gray-brown
feathers flecked with light. Or the duck itself,
a muddy brown, eddying along pond edge.
Camouflage, as in *camoufler*, the French verb
for *to disguise*. Or *camouflet*, as in *whiff of smoke*.
Entering the aviary, you saw it first—a dabbling teal,
scarcely distinguishable from foliage. *Duck*, I said
and pointed, quacked. And like that, it was gone.
How language dawns slowly, then all at once.
The dry, whitish lid working its way, reptilelike,
up the bird's eye. This isn't really about the duck,
the pointing. The point is that I saw you seeing
a creature for the first time—paused motionless
on the bridge, bits of debris shifting underfoot.
Every day you make some new utterance—*ball,
more, meow*—closing the space between the world
you live in and your name for it. Surprise. Hunger.
Spoon. Or maybe this is about the duck—you, me,
that dappled afternoon. The tender, wrecked moment
before the duck was a duck, when it was nothing
but a whiff of smoke blown across water, which
all of us were once. One time you saw a duck
on a pond, a green-winged teal, and it was the first
time such a thing ever existed, light startled
off its back as it slid noiselessly across the water,
bill riffling beneath the surface, turning this way,
that, searching for something to eat, something
we could not see but knew all the same was there.

One

MOTHERSALT

Like an object from space, birth language is a sign of alien life: *Mucus plug. Meconium.* Also the language of newborns, with its twisted syntax of sleepless nights and bleary, milk-washed mornings. *Rooting, latch. Fore-* and *hindmilk*. For now, this private lexicon of flutter kick, swim. What feels like a heart, tumbling through the body.

Increasingly, I lose my breath, caught in the close room of pregnancy. I imagined you were a rag doll, a belle. A beautiful boy. I braced myself for the impact of bone breaking through and woke longing for you—the certainty of your head, bobbing against my breast.

I am beautiful with you. I wear you emblazoned across my face, herald of the life to come. Sometimes a hand appears, heavy with gold, to beckon the way through. A garland of marigolds, eyes opened endlessly into this new light. How one face leads to the next. The red thread of your days, stitched through mine. Our lives, so lovingly sutured.

Before me, the day sprawls. Its ungainly hours, a hamstrung gait. The morning casts an ugly light. I withdraw to repair my hair. I pass through the days, or perhaps they pass through me. Buttercup, red velvet. Coconut cream. I reek with wanting. Like yours, mine is a cavern of need.

We have been bringing home pears. The word *quince* is on my tongue, though we have none, are still eking out the last, sun-cracked peaches of summer. Every room, smeared with russet-colored light. Someone sets a pair of persimmons on the dining table, says, *Wait for them to ripen*. When they do, it will be silently, with the force of a season. The flesh, sliced with a paring knife, will fall open like a mouth.

The midwife slides the wand across my belly, and your face swerves into view, an otherworldly blur of white on black. You, dreaming in an amniotic sea. The image veers off-screen and returns: eye sockets, rib cage. Strange that I have not thought, until now, of love. *Love!* The heart, such a stubborn, cagey muscle. If I could just touch you, smell your unborn skin.

They say the cervix is a sleeve-shaped muscle with a cuff or lip. That it thins—the word is *effaces*—then dilates, like the pupil of an eye. Taking the whole world in or letting it out.

ON FORM

I became a mother and I began to write like a Japanese woman.

Which is to say: I began to write like myself—from the imaginary whence my mother's mother and her mother before her came.

Things That Are Distant Though Near: Festivals celebrated near the Palace. The zigzag path leading up to the temple of Kurama.

When I became a mother, my lines began to grow less regular, less sculpted—and this itinerant prose did not adhere to shapeliness.

Instead it spilled from birth into death and questions of beauty, arranging itself as it wished.

An artful, yet imperfect text.

And so I began to build strange, unkempt houses for my words to live in. Interior spaces without doors, only half-imagined windows, which opened to rooms where a person could wander, lost, for days.

It's no surprise this didn't happen earlier—in school, for instance, when a professor handed me a book of haiku.

Deeply Irritating Things: A man who discusses all sorts of subjects at random as though he knew everything.

Tell me about the form mothering takes on the page. Why it accumulates so—fragments, notes. A slow, painstaking assemblage.

And I found myself heavy with the days.

And my belly bulged with them.

And the days accreted like lines.

Things That Give a Clean Feeling: An earthen cup. A new metal bowl. The play of the light on water as one pours it into a vessel.

ON GESTATION AND BECOMING

The radiance, for a time, gathered around my body. Like the smooth, green skin of a pear, lightly pitted with brown.

And the fear, held in equal measure. One does everything in her power to keep the baby, to save it, and yet.

The fetus' skin, so thin at this stage, may not be touched, lest it pull from the body. A shroud, unraveled.

Strange, how what is closest most eludes us.

How I feel when I see an ungainly tree laden with pears, some large enough to hold, but not ready to be plucked or eaten.

Each unripe fruit, joined to branch by a tiny umbilicus.

And if one of these pears were pulled from the tree? Its future—a spent, snubbed thing. Left on the counter, it would shrivel, harden; eventually rot.

Milky eyes. Larynx, yet unused. The heart, her body's stubborn engine. The promise of delicate organs, jostling one another in the fight to become.

The tongue, working in the pit of the face.

DEAR BODY—

We all pass through death to come into life, though some of us merely pass.

She lost a baby before me. Also a sister. *Imagine*.

Hearing this story is like breathing air that has not been breathed for forty years. Afterward I go home. I light so many candles.

When I was born, she counted my fingers and toes, and then wept to see me alive. She looked down at me, cradled in her arms, and I was beautiful.

It's the light she remembers, she says. The slow, wonder-filled hours.

After giving birth, I woke every night soaked in milk—the front of my nightgown, the sheets. Damp stains on cotton, a shape that spreads.

The shape of her story, which I lived in but had no words for, though I wore it like a second skin.

We who begin in this way, surely we can taste it. The tang of melancholy, seeping through amniotic fluid.

Her body, bent over the sewing machine—and me, stirring inside. Stitched from bone, from the pound and yammer of machinery.

The needle's noisy whir. Ravenous, eating down the miles of grief.

Difficult beauty, they say, takes time. *What happens next is never ours to say*.

DEAR BODY—

What if inside this story is another story, just as inside every mother is a daughter—and a daughter inside her, and still another, nested forms reaching through time.

A hole in the ground and a tree in the hole, and a bird in the tree and an egg in the bird, and a hole— and a hole.

Like her, I remember the light: daily walks; loose, blowsy sunshine. The sky's deep purple.

The small, bright world she made for me. The rooms I moved through, hushed and familiar at bedtime.

Together, they became a kind of *knowing*: that this was a place in the world, and that within their embrace existed a space for me.

The world-as-holding, where each night I lay and looked into the dark, every moment a luminous ritual: the hour of brushing teeth, the hour of pajamas. The hour of bedtime stories and hour of darkness.

And then time's sudden, terrible magic—a swallowing, or maybe a collapse.

The days poured out in a continuous stream, disappearing as though through a sieve.

That tiny, precious world growing more and more distant, receding to a place I could no longer feel except as an ache.

Smaller and smaller, until it became a speck and then—nothing at all. A life, unmade.

And the green grass grew all around all around, and the green grass grew all around.

ON MOTHERING

Tell me again about mothering. About the form it takes.

Interruptions, fractured sleep. The weird circularity of the days, accreting toward some hazy, impenetrable distance.

After I left the birth bed, I began to want a poetry in which motherhood was not so much its subject matter but its growing medium—the infrastructural condition of the poet's feeling and speaking mind.

The self, no longer a contained or containable thing, became multiplicitous—an overspill.

Along with that, a darkening of the armpits, the knee and elbow flexes. Deepened sweat glands around the nipples and the appearance of a dark line, reaching from navel to groin.

Some days I feel monstrous. Chimeric. As though I am that impossible beast, that mother who also writes.

The writer-mother senses a particularly urgent need to define herself, even with whole portions of her physical and psychic life designated to another's development. At times, it steals from itself to feed itself.

When I published my first book, a beloved teacher gave me an air plant—elegant, spiderlike. *Like you, dear*, she said. *That impossible thing.*

For a mother to be wholly a mother while being a writer and not an angel would create a new literature.

DEAR BODY—

I want to tell you a story, but I don't know how to begin.

I was afraid of saying *no*. I went in uninformed and inclined to please. I was concerned with doing birth correctly, whatever that meant.

Push! Push! Push! The nurses' shouting, the force of their insistence, though birth was a distant country, and I was stranded from its shore.

Mostly I remember the glare of overhead lights.

There was a doctor I had never seen. There was a battery of nurses and technicians whose faces and names I don't remember. There was, at one point, a midwife whose face I recognized, but then she was gone.

The room flooded with strangers, a rush of surgical masks and then, somehow, the baby.

I heard a faint cry, like the high, fluted call of a bird. Two notes, one slightly higher than the first, thin pitches rising then falling.

They placed her on my chest, and as I held her, pink and unblinking, I looked down and thought, *What now?*

Nurses moved briskly around the room, then they took her away. Suddenly the room was very quiet.

I wanted to be held, but there was no one. Only the far-off sound of beeping monitors.

I was afraid to leave the hospital. I had fallen so far out of my life, there appeared to be no way home.

Each time she woke, fitful and whimpering, I was gripped by a new form of loss.

On the morning of the third day, I sat in a vinyl chair, arms washed in midwinter light. Tentatively, I touched her tiny, cuffed hands. She opened her eyes and yawned.

We begin, and then we begin again.

The first thing she did when the midwife set her on my chest was to pull herself toward my nipple.

The tiny muscle working in her temple as she suckled, eyes gray and filmy from that other world.

A hungry child, but not exceptionally so. *Disoriented*, that's the word.

Midday blurred to evening, followed by an endless, milk-lit dawn.

We seldom left the apartment, each hour marked by the clanking of the radiator.

Senses locked on a single set of stimuli: tiny voice, piercing cry.

Each whimper, amplified a hundredfold. The constant feeding—a tether of human need.

When I did emerge, dazed, it was as though from a cocoon, organs dissolved into sticky fluid.

A roaring in the ears.

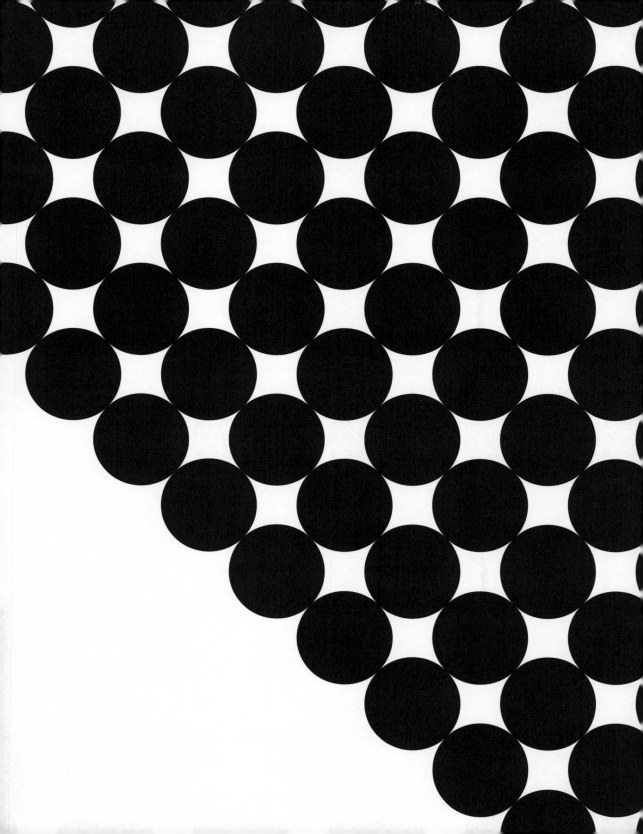

Two

MOTHERSALT

If the body goes rogue; turns against itself. If, between breaths, all I hear is the crunch of body against brick. If I am both body and brick. If my breath, stoppered in the throat, is a room without release. If you too are struggling, fists against face, fighting to be free.

They call this false labor, but to me it is real, each surge a brilliant orb—steely, white-hot—pulsing in the center of the solar system. Labor is a temple with many faces. In it, I discover my own. If pain is a house, I want to live in it fully—to throw the windows wide and let the light stream in. To examine the locks, pry open the hasps so every sash can be lifted.

I wake with a bullet between my teeth, grinning. The moon hangs in my hair like a flash of lightning. I am the body fantastic, dripping with silver and night sweats. Come near, come near. I am swollen with the bounty of fall. I crackle, I charge. My hair rises from the roots. Muscles lit with fire, I throw my big-bellied challenge to the sky.

When I close my eyes, I imagine your body's dark mass, crowning. Like staring at an eclipse in a sea of upturned faces. How the light grew starched without warning. The visible world, at once unfamiliar and disconcertingly without depth.

ON BEWILDERMENT

What I remember: the bright lights of the birthing ward; the scramble of nurses and respiratory techs rushing around the room as I lay on the bed, drugged and disoriented.

A nagging sadness, that I cannot remember the exact moment of her birth.

Why I have been talking to doulas and midwives and doctors and nurses, and even a kindly reproductive psychiatrist in Austin.

Maybe it's not facts I'm after so much as form. A container for this birth—its lapses and failures.

I felt defeated as I pushed. I wanted to take my laboring self out of that room, away from all those shouting strangers. I remember the light in my eyes.

A complete failure in the magnet, the compass, the scale.

Perhaps why I gasped, *Where am I?* when the time came. When what I really wanted to know was *what is happening?* and *will I survive?*

Nothing irradiates the self more powerfully than birth. The body, a howl in the dark.

The lie about birth is that it is a singular, isolated occurrence. That once you are done with it, it has done with you.

When perhaps it is more of a bloom or smear.

Long after the act is complete, birth lives on in our bodies, persisting like an enchantment—or a bad dream, depending.

BAD BIRTH: A RETROSPECTIVE

Perhaps the past is always trembling inside the present, whether or not we sense it.
—Doireann Ní Ghríofa

A poetics of haunting means a return to haunted places. It means choosing to tell the story from the beginning.

Women drugged without consent, strapped to the operating table or tied onto labor cots to keep them from clawing themselves.

Newborns dragged from their mothers' bodies, pincer-gripped by metal forceps. Sluggish from morphine, comatose or unable to breathe.

When I talk about birth in America, I am not talking about infants in starched linen, cooing in the delivery ward.

History—that trauma which will not forget us.

How many mothers, after giving birth, feel like a ghost in their own story? Trapped in its own ongoingness, birth becomes a fugue, a story that resists its own ending.

We need to develop our ability to identify the truth-claims of obstetrics for what they are and for what they seek to resist or deny about women.

Not long ago, laboring women were shaved, given enemas, sedated with morphine, and restrained with leather cuffs.

Twilight sleep, widely used in American hospital births beginning in the early 1900s, caused delirium, vivid hallucinations, and psychosis. It also induced memory loss.

How many of our mothers gave birth this way? Eyes wrapped in gauze, wrists rubbed raw from a struggle they would not remember.

In some ways, childbirth has the hallmarks of a good story (exposition, rising action, climax, and resolution), but just because a baby has been delivered doesn't mean the story is resolved.

You can build a good story around a bad one, but the ugliness persists—spreading underground, out of sight.

Maybe this bad story wants us to tell it over again, trying to get it right.

We cannot fight old power in old power terms only. The only way we can do it is by creating another whole structure that touches every aspect of our creation, at the same time as we are resisting.

de·liv·er | \ di-ˈli-vər, dē- \ **(transitive verb) 1 : to set free :** At first, I paced up and down in a gown that did not close at the back, trying but failing to Progress Labor. **2a : to take and hand over to or leave for another : CONVEY :** When they induced me, it was with jagged, spiky contractions. The fear: an eerie, bottlenecked sensation. Bent into a C-shape, I shivered from the epidural's sudden chill. **b : HAND OVER, SURRENDER :** Handled in this way, birth becomes managed, procedural. **c : to send, provide, or make accessible to someone electronically :** Later I request my medical records but, reading them, find no trace of myself. **3a (1) : to assist (a pregnant female) in giving birth :** The second time, I arrive in active labor, breathing hard and zeroed by contractions. The midwife kneels on the floor beside me, hands firm on my back. **(2) : to aid in the birth of :** *Take it low,* the doula says, *she's coming.* **b : to give birth to :** When I close my eyes, I see my vulva, stretched and swollen, its purplish red—and in the center, the dark of her head. **4 : SPEAK, SING, UTTER :** My body, fighting to deliver despite itself. *That band of scar tissue*, the doula says. *If only we'd known.* Dear Body— I want to say. Tell me your story. **5 : to send (something aimed or guided) to an intended target or destination :** They say most mothers want a natural birth but fail because of inadequate labor support. A third of all births end in C-section because of Failure to Progress. **6a : to bring (something, such as votes) to the support of a candidate or cause :** *Our vision is that every pregnant person should have an empowering birthing experience. We seek to empower birthing people to claim agency over their bodies.* **b : to come through with : PRODUCE :** *Bring it low*, the doula says, *and PUSH.* **(intransitive verb) : to produce the promised, desired, or expected results :** Time to birth a new narrative. To put our bodies back in the story, and the story back into our lives.

DEAR BODY—

At my second birth, I arrive in active labor, contractions barreling down my body.

I refuse the stares. I refuse the wheelchair.

Because the thing about stories is that they go on. In this way, writing and birth are both iterative processes.

We begin, and then we begin again.

I am livid with birth, stumble-stepping down the hallway, L&D staff crowding me with clipboards and monitors.

Ready for the epidural? a nurse keeps asking—and I refuse. Once, twice, three times. Also I refuse the bed, the gown, the towels.

I sink to my knees, wracked by contractions so strong, it's a kind of dismemberment. I no longer know myself, but I know this pain—or maybe it knows me.

The steely force of her body against mine, each surge throwing itself headlong down the throat of the one that follows—

I lurch to the bathroom, and the bag of waters ruptures across the floor.

It's her! the doula cries, and they rush me to the bed, help me kneel on all fours; and then the pushing, the constriction, and—*oh!*—the inside-out burst of her body emerging from mine—the slippery, muscular force of a life spilling into the next.

And the afterpains. And the cramped, shuddery bladder; the heat of a world, collapsing.

Patient initially pushed in hands and knees position. Fetal heartbeat auscultated to 70-80 bmp with slow crowning of fetal head. Patient repositioned to left side lying position. Lidocaine infiltrated. Pediatric team due to intermittent deceleration between 70s and 120s bpm. Midline episiotomy performed with delivery of fetal head followed immediately by shoulder and body. **Baby** *placed on maternal abdomen* **and** *midline episiotomy repaired under lidocaine anesthesia.* **Mother** *and infant stable and bonding. Placenta* **delivered** *spontaneously and* **intact.**

Everything female in me has broken. I've come unmoored from the hours, crawl into pockets of time where there are none. The weeks disappear like a dropped stitch. The sun lifts its skirts and runs off with the days.

I'm shot through with clotted milk. There's a demon in the ointment, electric orange. Each night, a broken bone, crookedly splinted into sleep. I scrabble after the hours, caught in the cogs of time's machinations.

I watch as you surface from sleep's sticky layers—my breasts swollen, tingling with milk. The miracle of multiplication: the more I give, the more I have. From fullness to fullness. From nothing, *everything*.

At last, we have reached the end, which is not an end, but an interval. Around us, labor takes on different dimensions. Pain builds a new roof. You breathe through the hours, little whispers in and out of just-birthed lungs. The crown of your head, rung with light. Even now, your body, formed in another realm, bears the shape of the invisible world. My body, though no longer gestating, feels fuller than ever.

AFTER/BIRTH

In the final stage of labor, the afterbirth is severed from the uterine wall and delivered without fanfare. Remarkably, it leaves no scar.

After I delivered the placenta, a nurse held it up for me to see, a thick fleshy mass that looked like it belonged on the inside. Shockingly meaty, a dark purple red.

We think of this organ as signaling the end of labor, but in a way, it marks the beginning—and may even be the entire story.

Soon after conception, the embryo burrows into the uterine lining and breaks into the mother's capillaries with narrow, fingerlike columns.

As the placenta forms, bits of the baby's DNA slip into the mother's bloodstream—a fraught, interpenetrating intimacy.

If the mother does not defend herself against this onslaught of need, she will not survive, which is to say that a fetus's life is wholly dependent on its mother's ability to fight back.

With this writing, I feel the afterbirth's vestigial presence, reminding me of a reality in which both mother and child are satiated, fed.

Like you, dear. That impossible thing.

Perhaps what my body was mourning in those early days, when the baby whimpered for milk, and I felt only a sense of failure.

Life is a series of wombs, the doula says, *a series of interconnected passages*.

Then she offered placenta encapsulation, which I declined. Though later I did wonder.

Thinking of my childhood cat, who birthed her first litter in my bed, tearing the sac from each kitten's body with her teeth, gnawing every scrap of placenta and membrane until not a trace was left.

What would it mean to swallow birth whole? To absorb it back into the body?

Writing is a process of discovery, a struggle to reconstruct oneself and heal the sustos resulting from woundings, traumas, racism, and other acts of violence que hechan pedazos nuestras almas, split us, scatter our energies, and haunt us.

If birth is a story, then what is it saying? And who will listen?

DEAR BODY—

If birth is a story, maybe I can write it backward and forward.

Maybe I can gather the threads and weave them into a nest, in remembrance of how things could have been.

In another life, I wake in the middle of the night and stumble to the bathroom. Behind me trails a thick, wet river.

In this other life, the house fills with mothers who come from war, who have lost homes and countries.

Mothers who gave birth in the desert behind barbed wire. Who stood in line for milk and put their babies in empty washbasins to save them from dust storms.

In this other world, they crowd into the room, holding me as I break apart.

She's coming, I can feel her, she's *here*—bound by a thick, jelly-slick umbilical cord, which we gently unwind from her neck.

It's her! we say and press her to my chest. We massage her vigorously, the umbilical cord pulsating like a living thing, and she is blue then purple then pink and finally a wild red, and at last she gurgles and begins to cry.

In this other world, I surge with colostrum, and the drops of this sticky new life are thick and yellow, beading on the nipple.

I cradle her, marveling at her hands, the pale crescents of her fingernails. My tiny, exquisite miracle.

For we have passed through death and emerged wet and bleeding.

In this way, we are torn apart and stitched back together.

Three

ON WEANING

Today I boarded a plane. Where does one body begin and the other end?

A shock, that I am leaving it all behind—freeways, blocky tracts of gray. The merged self we make: mother, mouth, milk.

As a mother, sometimes I feel atmospheric in nature. Such diminishment, to be merely a body—yet also a relief.

I watch as the sea's blue-gray edges lift and lay themselves down. A ceaseless flattening.

In the end, we all come to water.

My breasts, weeping milk. Marking the hours that cleave us.

The first night, I wake to a twinge in my left breast. I huddle over the bathroom sink, pump pressed to chest. Nipple elongated, silky with milk.

How tightly we are bound. By the hours, sliding past. My body's secretions.

With no one else around, I tip my chin and drink it down. A single warm, creamy mouthful. I am drinking myself in, a new sensation.

The next night, I do the same.

The third night, I do not wake up. My body is no longer the full, fertile tide it once was. Impossible, that I could leave all this behind.

Continents, seas—the ocean's blue sprawl, its restless churn.

At takeoff, I feel the air around me resist. My belly tugs tight, as though tied to land by an umbilical cord.

In flight, I lose all sense of where one body ends and the next begins.

SHELTERING

Ready or not, here we are. We've been lost and found,
      gone underground. We've been Stuck in the Mud,
pounded flowers to pulp. We've traced ourselves
      in chalk, watched our bodies turn to brilliant dust.

Something comes into the world calling disorder, disorder—
      ordered home, we're baking. You peer into the oven.
I don't know how much longer, I say, lost, too in this
      interminable landscape. Around us, the death toll rises.

The pandemonium, you call it. *Enculturation*, they say,
      bringing a child into language—from raw and unformed
to browned. Somewhere in the desert, my great-grandfather
      lifts a stone from a dry creek bed. Sui meaning *water*,

suiseki as in *viewing stones*. He touches the rough,
      chiseled edges. Gently sets it on end. For days,
he contemplates its dimensions. A desolate island,
      perhaps—blueprint of some past or future grief.

How many times have we made life from dust? Unearthed,
      we've found the white of bones, sound of singing. *At the end
of my suffering there was a door*. One day we will reenter
      the house of the living. You chant rhymes, write your name

for the first time. It's spring again. With your sister,
      you pick wild irises with gold veins, bellflowers with red
and yellow striations. Your bodies—so beloved, sometimes
      I mistake one for the other—climb into bed beside me.

I was once afraid—I still am, but every night
      the sun sets, and in the gloaming, a star—
or is it light from a plane—blinks on—

SPRING

I took the baby to the Japanese garden and she stood under the cherry blossoms.

Flowers at their fullest, beauty undercut by the tinge of their passing. Perfectly manicured, but in a delicate, rangy way.

The trees held their breath, waiting.

Today I understood for the first time why people go to see the cherry blossoms. Why there are whole festivals dedicated to their viewing.

Why my grandmother wanted her bed turned to face the tree in her garden, in full bloom the day she died.

We stop to watch a trail of ants. Their bodies gleam blackly against rock. They are so tentative, so industrious.

We watch them touch their antennae to one another and carry on.

The minor and the hidden, the ephemeral.

I point at the koi, telling her I like the black and gold one best. Teaching her what is pleasing and what is not.

The wind stirs, and a petal lands in the baby's hair: a benediction. Her hand on the tree's silver trunk. Patches of gray, like skin.

A moment before there were no blossoms. A moment hence there will be no blossoms.

How poetic, I think to myself, to die on that day.

> *Look. Oh, look.*
> *All is clear, openly revealed.*
> *This countenance, this mien.*

ON MEMORY

Today I am thinking about the mind's relationship to time, and how my daughters are old enough now that there are things they do not remember.

In other words, they have acquired the ability to forget.

In conversation, I find myself saying, *When you were a baby,* and *when you were little*, and the look they give me—

it's as though I'm telling them about someone else's life. Which, in a way, I am.

The hours spent in half sleep, before they knew their hands were their own—watched them drift in front of their unrecognizing faces.

How it had felt to be wordless, completely of the physical world—that even before my body was an instrument for language it had been an instrument for memory.

You were blue, I say. *The umbilical cord was wrapped around your neck. They took you away, and then they brought you back.*

Her face fills with questions, like water running into a glass. *Why did they take me away? Where did I go? How long until they brought me back?*

With this telling, I am weaving her an origin story—one, I realize, in which I am incidental.

Her dark, rabbity eyes as she lay on my breast after birth, rosy and womb-shaped.

Birth work, the doula reminds me, *is a lifelong process*. I weep to hold these memories, charged with the responsibility of remembering what she does not.

Each drawn-out day and fractured, contraction-gutted night. My belly, a luminous bulge that torqued this way, then that.

How each child, obstructed in some way—one by the entanglement of the umbilical cord, the other by a thick, unforgiving cuff of scar tissue—emerged, roaring with light.

Then the moments after. My belly draped slackly as I stood to pee.

Moments worth remembering, though in recalling them, I risk altering them. Episodic memory, a tricky, shape-shifting thing.

The least contaminated memory might exist in the brain of a patient with amnesia—in the brain of someone who cannot contaminate it by remembering it.

The perfect memory, forged in the newborn's mind before she knows enough to forget. The tug of soft palate against nipple. The first swallow, followed by the next, that reflex that leads to life.

A kind of grace, that she does not remember this moment enough to lose it.

LAST DAY IN LAGUNA

If only I could capture the hours, the bright
        bauble of the day. The walk to Anita Street Beach,
the gentle slope of pavement past clapboard
        houses. One red-painted door, then another.
At the family beach house, a glass fish swivels
        on a string; a garnet-eyed owl keeps its watch
from the corner of the garden. Inside, you find
        a ship in a bottle, a collection of songbooks
and ceramic angels, shelved under your great-
        grandfather's graduation portrait.
Someday, you'll want to know where you come
        from, and I'll point to this memory:
you, at two, running along the side of the house—
        sand-streaked, shivering, hosed clean
at day's end. What we leave behind: a line of white
        stones, picked from a bed of rocks. A chair
with the imprint of your body. Our shadows
        stretched across asphalt: you, arms swinging,
high on your dad's shoulders; me, seven months
        pregnant, trailing behind. I'm trying to hold
this memory for you, trying to catch every
        last detail: your sleepy face pressed to mine,
low murmurs in the gathering dark. I leave
        the door ajar and move through the house,
tidying what's left of the day's debris. Scattered
        pillows, blocks, the last traces of play, erased
as I steal to bed, climb wooden steps to where
        your father waits with a book—nightstand,
lamp glow, holding the last precious light of the day.

TODAY

Today you saw a giraffe for the first time and said, *Gi'affe! Gi'affe!*

Today you pointed at the sky and said, *Ocean*, and when I said *sky*, you pointed again and said, *No. Ocean.*

Today I said, *I love you, darling*, and you said, *I love you Fancy Nancy.*

Today you put your hands on my cheeks and turned my face toward you. *Look at me. Look at Me*, you said. *No. Biting.*

Today you walked around the house patting a doll on the back saying, *That's okay baby, that's okay.*

Today you showed me Butterfly Legs and Bear Walk and Tip Toes.

Today you rode a merry-go-round for the first time.

Today you said, *Can I whisper to you*, and pressed your ear against mine. *Today we're on a hike. I found a stick, we ate some crackers, we found a door.*

Today you said your heart felt hopeful.

Today you said you wanted a pink cake with chocolate writing and strawberries for your birthday.

Today you said, *But my cake didn't have chocolate writing*, and I said, *Well, at least it had strawberries.*

ON AMBIVALENCE

Maternal ambivalence, it's called, and I have to say: some days, just saying the words dispels the darkness I live in.

Though my mother, when I tell her about this feature of contemporary mothering, tells me she hopes my children never hear me say such a thing.

In *Motherhood*, Sheila Heti says parenting and art each take up all your time, so why would a person ever try to do both?

Perhaps the reason my writing life is characterized by low-level anxiety, and I sometimes feel that if I forget to take deep breaths, I might not make it through.

A sickly yellow buzz, underpinning my thoughts. The clutch of panic in my throat.

How to make a home for feelings that are so unhomely? To bring the unloving into the space of the home? Our most frightening, unheimlich selves.

What is "allowable" for a woman?

Birth and motherhood upended everything and fractured my sense of self as a constant, whole entity. Doubled and broke me open and split me into two selves and then gave selfhood to one and wrenched that self away.

Some days, birth feels so far away, like a lost language or a face I've begun to forget.

This morning, I lay in bed listening to the toddler walk into the bathroom and take off her diaper, then climb onto the toilet seat. Then silence, followed by the sound of her climbing off the stool and flushing.

And I think, *Have I woken from a dream?* and *maybe I'm not so ill-suited to this, after all.*

And they clamber into bed with me—these lean, untethered things, who belong only to themselves.

Though as infants, they belonged mostly to me, and I to them.

And I wait for the melancholy of this epiphany, but there is only the tug of the future, and I feel, for the first time in days, *happy*.

ON WORLDS THAT LEAVE US

How easy to lift her into the crib, to hand her a cup. To watch her pull long sips from the spout.

Watching her, I am only faintly aware of the ritual that once sequestered us in a world of our own making: latch, nipple, skin.

The slow drift from wakefulness to sleep.

Now that she is weaned, how easy to live around the edges of that world. As though it never existed.

Though of course it did—and still does, its shadows emerging in bedtime's hush.

As in the moments after childbirth, when I felt a sudden coldness: strangely alone in my body, carrying not two heartbeats, but one.

How worlds create then leave us. *A swallowing, or maybe a collapse.*

I am thinking of the nursery in Richmond my family once owned, roses run wild in glass houses.

The touch of Oxford in my in-laws' English.

The weary boulevards of Vientiane. The streets of Paris.

How world-haunted we all are.

The baby, now a toddler, bath-damp hair against my cheek.

The worlds that wait. And those that linger—that leave us gasping for breath.

TODAY

Today you told me you're me, only smaller.

Today you told me you love your teacher and her beautiful, hangy bun and her beautiful skirt and her cape that she always wears.

Today you clapped your hands to your ears and said, *Peek-a-boo!*

Today you told me 1+1=11.

Today you ate all your food, then patted the inside of the bowl to check.

Today you nursed for the last time, then fell asleep in my arms.

Today you said you love me more than you can even describe.

Today you said your favorite part of the Pledge of Allegiance is *witches stand*.

Today you touched your chest and said your name for the first time.

Today you asked what comes after white hair. *Maybe rainbow,* you said.

Today you said, *When I grow up I'm going to marry Mama*.

Today you read one of my poems and said it was a silly one, because when you read it you could hear me using my important person voice.

ON COLLAPSE

I once shared a table with a person whom I will not name, who looked at me in a way that made me feel foreign, even to myself, and asked why, if I was raised overseas, I spoke such good English.

Why do you feel comfortable saying this to me?

The space suddenly stripped of its easy, familial feeling. The rest of the family, cutting strawberries in the kitchen.

A constriction in the throat, an ugly orange buzz in the room. As if someone had pushed the *mute* button: the children's voices suddenly silent in the other room, the *scritch-scritch* of the dog's paws on the glass sliding door, weirdly without sound.

Certain moments send adrenaline to the heart, dry out the tongue, and clog the lungs.

Some people are born into the *I* and feel it is their birthright to say *I this* and *I that*, but others are made to believe that *I* doesn't matter, especially in relation to *They*, which means our coming into selfhood is tentative and sometimes belated.

Why, when the moment collapsed, taking with it my sense of *I*-ness, I felt so powerless.

In infancy, we come to see ourselves by mimicking the actions of others. Why a baby might wave with her palm turned toward her—because that is how others acknowledge her. Or why, recognizing her likeness in a photo, a toddler might say, *That's you!*

Why, when another person swallows the space, I can no longer see myself. Blood hammering in my ears; the air sucked from the room.

My only response was to become forced and brittle, asserting my edges but failing to exist as anything but surface glare.

The sharpness of her voice. The glazed unknowingness of her affect.

The moment's betrayal, like an egg crushed on the face. Yolk smeared across the mouth, in the hair— ugly and shaming.

Why do you feel comfortable saying this to me?

The rest of the family, slicing fruit at the counter. Listening, but not speaking.

ON FILLING THE SPACE

What is life but a series of containers, and what is a mother but one who fills them? The hours as they pass. The inside of a child's mouth. The cup, the bowl.

I touch my pelvic crest and tell them where the fetus grows. I teach them the words: *Labia. Vulva.*

Womanhood is the country I come from, a home I reach back for to reproduce, recreate, replenish.

In my own mother's body, I was a fullness. Her skin, tight like the surface of a drum; a dark, wandering line stretched from navel to pelvis.

My body's slow transformation, when I became all protrusion, belly thrust so far forward my spine curved. My hair, thick and glossy.

To grow fat with joy.

A friend sits at my table, swallowing every bite hungrily, and when I ask whom she usually eats with, she says she only eats alone.

Another friend hosts me for dinner, and afterward all I can say is, *I'm so full!* and I mean it.

What comes to us empty goes away full.

When my daughters are angry, I teach them to say, *I need some space*. I tell them it is a kinder response than *go away*.

Not *I* after all, pushing into the space. Not *I*, but *we*—space as offering, rather than refusal.

To mother the space is to make it full.

I come from fullness. I am fat with joy.

LATE SPRING

Yesterday I took the baby to the tea garden, and the cherry trees had all gone to green.

She pressed her cheek to a flagstone and lay down, like she was going to sleep.

She pressed her body to the rock and grew very still.

She became a stone.

I saw her lying there, and she was no longer a baby.

She stood up and said, *I want to go home*.

INSTAX: A NEW LYRIC

One winter I bought my daughter an Instax camera. Through the lens, the magnolia tree in front of our house looked taller than in real life, its creamy whites and magentas more lovely.

This is so beautiful, she said, and pressed the shutter release.

The "room" of the camera may have shrunk, but [it] retains, in its name, a reference to that magical space one originally occupied: the dark room where one went to receive an illuminated version of reality.

Photographs show not the presence of the past but the pastness of the present.

Is it possible for an image to be an elegy? For a photograph, as it captures the light of a lost moment, to be anything *but*?

The more interesting abrasions are not of stone but of flesh. Through photographs we follow in the most intimate, troubling way the reality of how people age.

One day she will say, *I can't believe how young you were.* Looking at me now, you would not know I was once a small child in overalls with blue yarn in my hair.

The smearing effect of time, memory. Distance and sun exposure.

Dear one, do you ever feel as I do that the walls of our home are tilted? That we are sliding on an invisible axis toward some undefinable point on the horizon?

One day I will look and see that she is no longer a baby, and from the vantage of the future, our lives will appear to be no more than a shedding of selves through the years.

While pregnant, I became obsessed with the passage of time. Something about the marks it made on my skin as it stretched past.

A sort of umbilical cord links the body of the photographed thing to my gaze: light is here a carnal medium, a skin I share with anyone who has been photographed.

What I remember about my own mother: some days I returned from school and the floors gleamed.

She was everything, but she was also invisible.

Once I left a pair of scissors on the floor, and she cut her foot open, trailing blood to the bathroom. How it feels as the frame that holds your life falls to pieces.

One day I will forget how high the ceilings were. How their exposed beams collected shadows, which drifted across the walls in complex, shifting prisms.

The light of those long-ago hours. As though *filtered through a dream or a halftone screen.*

To document the light it is to catch the quality of time as it streams past.

Photography is an elegiac art, a twilight art.

We live in the presence of another world, faces lit from the inside.

Look Mama, she says, pressing the viewfinder to her eye. Her fingers find the shutter button, and the world explodes in a flash.

Bodies bleached by sun, faces haloed in gauzy light. How joy effervesces—and what is lost in the glow.

NOTES

"On Form" incorporates language adapted from Leonard Koren's *Wabi-Sabi for Artists, Designers, Poets & Philosophers* (Imperfect Publishing, 2008) and Sei Shōnagon's *The Pillow Book of Sei Shōnagon*, translated by Ivan Morris (Columbia University Press, 2018).

"Dear Body— [We all pass through death]" refers to Bernard Bosanquet's thinking on difficult beauty, as referenced in Chloé Cooper Jones' memoir *Easy Beauty* (Avid Reader Press, 2022). The poem ends with a line from Molly McCully Brown and Susannah Nevison's epistolary poetry collection *In the Field Between Us* (Persea Books, 2020).

"On Mothering" includes adapted language from Miranda Field's essay "Miranda Field on Fanny Howe," which appears in *Women Poets on Mentorship: Efforts and Affections*, edited by Arielle Greenberg and Rachel Zucker (University of Iowa Press, 2008), as well as from Barbara Einzig's "First Things First: *notes toward a discovery of* Being a Mother Being a Writer," printed in *The Grand Permission: New Writings on Poetics and Motherhood*, edited by Patricia Dienstfrey and Brenda Hillman (Wesleyan University Press, 2003). Other material is from *Childbirth Wisdom from the World's Oldest Societies* by Judith Goldsmith (Congdon & Weed, 1984).

"On Bewilderment" contains lines from the essay "Bewilderment" by Fanny Howe, originally presented as a talk at the Poetics & Readings Series at New College in San Francisco and later published in *HOW2*, vol. 1:1, 1999. With special thanks to Jennifer S. Cheng.

"Bad Birth: A Retrospective" is inspired by Jane Wong's work on the poetics of haunting, characterized as the deliberate choice "to move toward haunted places." The poem also references material from Judith

Goldsmith's *Childbirth Wisdom from the World's Oldest Societies*; Deidre Cooper Owens' *Medical Bondage: Race, Gender, and the Origins of American Gynecology* (University of Georgia Press, 2017); Christiane Northrup's *Mother-Daughter Wisdom: Understanding the Crucial Link Between Mothers, Daughters, and Health* (Bantam, 2006); Henci Goer's paper "Cruelty in Maternity Wards: Fifty Years Later" (*The Journal of Perinatal Education*, vol. 19:3, 2010); and Neel Shah's "I'm an OB/GYN who attended thousands of deliveries before wondering why Americans give birth in bed" (*The Conversation*, January 8, 2020, theconversation.com). The poem also contains quotations from Audre Lorde's essay "The Uses of Anger: Women Responding to Racism," published in *Sister Outsider* (Crossing Press, 1984), and the epigraph is from Doireann Ní Gríofa's *A Ghost in the Throat* (Biblioasis, 2021).

"Deliver" takes its form and definitions from the Merriam-Webster Dictionary. It also includes language from the mission statements of the organization Black Women Birthing Justice and the Roots of Labor Birth Collective, which can be found on their respective websites. Proceeds from this book will be donated to these and similar organizations in support of birthing and reproductive justice.

"After/birth" references information from Peter W. Nathanielsz's *A Time to Be Born: The Life of the Unborn Child* (Oxford University Press, 1994) and the *Radiolab* episode "Everybody's Got One" (WNYC Studios, August 20, 2021). It also contains a quotation adapted from Gloria Anzaldúa's *Light in the Dark/Luz en Lo Oscuro: Rewriting Identity, Spirituality, Reality* (Duke University Press, 2015).

"Dear Body— [If birth is a story]" owes a special debt of gratitude to Yae Wada for her life and stories. And to Motoko Higaki, Chu Sakai, Masuye Tabuchi, Toyo Iwai, Sachiko Higaki, and Shigeko Sakai, for their powerful ancestral presence.

"Sheltering" contains lines from Louise Glück's "The Wild Iris" and "Witchgrass," which appear in *The Wild Iris* (Ecco Press, 1992). The notion of enculturation as bread baking is from the essay "The Memory of the Senses: Historical Perception, Commensal Exchange, and Modernity" by C. Nadia Seremetakis, published in *Visualizing Theory: Selected Essays from V.A.R., 1990-1994*, edited by Lucien Taylor (Routledge, 1994).

"On Memory" includes quotations from *Ongoingness: The End of a Diary* by Sarah Manguso (Graywolf Press, 2015).

"Today," an (ongoing) multipart poem, owes a debt of gratitude to Rachel Khong.

"On Ambivalence" contains a quotation from *MOTHERs* by Rachel Zucker (Counterpath, 2014).

"On Collapse" includes language from *Citizen: An American Lyric* by Claudia Rankine (Graywolf Press, 2014).

"On Filling the Space" takes a line from *The Year of Blue Water* by Yanyi (Yale University Press, 2019).

"Spring" includes lines adapted from Soetsu Yanagi's *The Beauty of Everyday Things*, translated by Michael Brase (Penguin Books, 2018); Andrew Juniper's *Wabi Sabi: The Japanese Art of Impermanence* (Tuttle Publishing, 2003); and Leonard Koren's *Wabi-Sabi for Artists, Designers, Poets & Philosophers*.

"Instax: A New Lyric" adapts language from numerous texts, including *On Photography* by Susan Sontag (Farrar, Straus and Giroux, 1978); *Light in the Dark Room: Photography and Loss* by Jay Prosser (University of Minnesota, 2005); *Camera Lucida: Reflections on Photography* by Roland Barthes, translated by Richard Howard (Farrar, Straus and Giroux, 1981); *Ghost Image* by Hervé Guibert, translated by Robert Bononno (University of Chicago Press, 1996); and the essay "She Is a Radical" by Tara Villalba and Lola Mondragón in *Revolutionary Mothering: Love on the Front Lines*, edited by Alexis Pauline Gumbs, China Martens, and Mai'a Williams (PM Press, 2016).

ACKNOWLEDGMENTS

Grateful acknowledgment to the editors of the following journals and anthologies, in which earlier versions of these poems first appeared: *A Gathering of the Tribes, ANMLY, Braving the Body, CALYX, Columbia Journal, Connotation Press: An Online Artifact, DUSIE, GUEST, Literary Mama, Los Angeles Review, Mass Poetry, Memorious, MiGoZine, Poetry Northwest, Prairie Schooner, Indiana Review, Spoon River Poetry Review, SUSPECT, Taos Journal of Poetry and Art, The Journal, The Offing, The Yale Review, They Rise Like a Wave: An Anthology of Asian American Women Poets, Washington Square Review, West Trestle Review*, and *Your Impossible Voice*.

And with thanks to Bateau Press for publishing the chapbook *Notes on the Birth Year*, this book's first incarnation.

To the many artists, poets, researchers, activists, and birth practitioners who helped make a way where there was none: thank you. Truly, it takes a village.

To Jasmine San, Kirstin Soares, Maria Baalbaki, Shawna Okamoto, Jasmine Marotta-Jaenecke, Molly Geisler, Mariko Jensen, Kristin Lasseter, Lily Bastian, Aaron Mochizuki, Charissa Pomrehn, Yae Wada, and Nadia Cooper; thank you for sharing your life and work with me. Special thanks to Allison Ledwith Glubiak.

To the gracious women at Blossom Birth & Family, Bellingham Birth Center, Nightingale Birth Center, and the San Francisco Doula Group.

To Carey Salerno, Alyssa Neptune, and the rest of the amazing staff at Alice James Books.

To my beloved Weird Moms, Kind Rigor poets, and all the brilliant folks at The Ruby.

To the South Bay Writers' Collective and my wonderful students at Left Margin LIT, without whom I never would have discovered this book's hidden form: *a nest, a spiral, a bloom*.

To Cheryl Zuffi, Ms. Melanie, Ms. Margarita, and everyone else who cared for me and my children by giving me the time I needed to write this book.

To Anna and Alice, my treasures. And to Mark—*it was always you*.

And of course, to my parents, whose lives have enabled my own.

RECENT TITLES FROM ALICE JAMES BOOKS

Alice James Books is committed to publishing books that matter. The press was founded in 1973 in Boston, Massachusetts to give women access to publishing. As a cooperative, authors performed the day-to-day undertakings of the press. The press continues to expand and grow from its formative roots, guided by its founding values of access, excellence, inclusivity, and collaboration in publishing. Its mission is to publish books that matter and preserve a place of belonging for poets who inspire us. AJB seeks to broaden our collective interpretation of what constitutes the American poetic voice and is dedicated to helping its artists achieve purposeful engagement with broad audiences and communities nationwide. The press was named for Alice James, sister to William and Henry, whose extraordinary gift for writing went unrecognized during her lifetime.

Designed by Tiani Kennedy

Printed by Versa Press